Contents

Walk

It is strongly recommended that walkers wear suitable clothing and footwear, appropriate to the walk and conditions that can sometimes be encountered on open moorland and exposed hillsides. This usually means walking boots, outer waterproof/windproof jacket and a type of walking trousers (**not jeans**) along with a warm sweater and other body clothing. A small day rucksack with some food/drink and your personal items are also strongly recommended.

The description of a route or track is not evidence of a right of way.
Compass bearings shown in this book are given as magnetic bearings.

It is recommended that a compass and the following map be used in conjunction with this book. Ordnance Survey Explorer No. OL1 The Peak District - Dark Peak Area

To help shorten the text the following abbreviations have been used throughout: -

PF = Public Footpath	**LT** = Left	**S** = Start
PB = Public Bridleway	**RT** = Right	**P** = Park
CP = Car Park	**RD** = Road	**FB** = Footbridge

The walks have been graded for difficulty with 1 being the easiest/flattest to 5 the most demanding in terms of ascents/descents: -
I hope you enjoy this selection of walks, which are spread throughout the Edale/Castleton areas. All are undulating but the majority are not too demanding, with excellent scenery and views from the hills. I hope you get as much pleasure from walking them as I did.

Brian Smailes

Walk 1: Castleton View Walk
Walk Time: 2hrs   **Distance 3.5miles/5.6km**
Start: GR. 149830 - Main CP in Castleton
A good scenic walk with a short moderate ascent up Treak Cliff.

1. Leaving the main **CP** in Castleton, turn **RT** and walk to the **CP** for Peak Cavern, turning **LT**. At the far side cross a stone bridge over the stream. Turn **RT** and ascend the narrowing **RD** between the houses to where it ends (1). Continue on a stony track and go through a gate. Keep the stone wall on your **RT** as you follow a narrow path sweeping round to a gate leading onto the minor **RD** (2).
2. Cross the minor **RD** near Speedwell Cavern and go between two stone posts and continue on the obvious narrow path as you ascend towards Treak Cliff Cavern. Go up the steps to Treak Cliff Cavern then ascend another set of steps past it before turning immediately **RT** to walk behind the building on a narrow ascending path. Going through a gate, it takes you over the hillside and through another gate onto the topside of the hill.
3. On the top of the hill, walk across the open grass area to another gate by Blue John Cavern (3) then turn **RT** on the access **RD**. Walk round to the **CP** for the cavern on the minor **RD**. Turn **RT** and continue descending the **RD** past the parking places to a turning area.
4. Go through a small gate at the far side and follow the now disused **RD**, with care, down to another gate. Go through that gate and continue now straight ahead, going down a small stone track to Mam Farm (4). As you reach the farm courtyard, turn **RT** over a stile and follow the winding track round and over another stile as it gently descends.
5. You emerge in a small open area surrounded by trees where you bear **LT** across to another path in the direction of the cement works in the distance. As you descend cross a stile and go down a flight of steps then through a gate by the farm there. You emerge in front of Knowlegates Farm (5) and go through a small gate.
6. Cross a stone step stile then over another stile by a 5-bar gate, now heading into Castleton. At a cattle grid, do not cross, but walk to the far side of it and cross the stile. Keep the brook on your **LT** as you walk back into Castleton (6). At the **RD**, turn **LT** and walk along to the **CP** in Castleton.

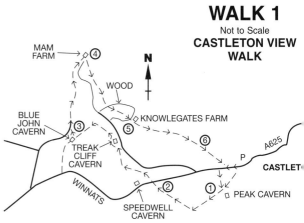

WALK 1
Not to Scale
CASTLETON VIEW WALK

Walk 2: Castleton Hills Circular

Walk Time: 2hrs   **Distance 3.9miles/6.3km**

Start: GR. 149830 - Main CP in Castleton

A steep ascent followed by a steady walk over high ground then steep descent.

1. Leave the main **CP** in Castleton and cross to walk between the 3 Roofs Café and the Blue John Jewellers. Continue between the shops and houses then keep the stream on your **RT** as you walk to the small stone bridge a short distance further.

2. At the bridge continue walking along the **RD**, which narrows further up, then at the top, walk onto the stony track and continue past the trees, going through a gate onto a narrow path by a stone wall. Continue round the crescent shaped path then halfway round; look for a feint grass track branching steeply **LT** up the hillside (1).

3. Continue ascending to the top and turn **RT** near the wire fence and walk over the open grass to the **RT** of some crags with trees on them. Continue past the crags, now on flatter ground, to a farm gate at the far end of the large field. Cross a stone step stile at the side of the gate and walk up between the two broken stone walls. At the end of the broken walls, continue ahead ascending the field in the same direction.

4. You come to a wooden 5-bar gate (2) with an opening at the side. Go through then over a stone step stile soon after onto a track. Turn **RT** here on a stony track between two stone walls. When you come to a bend in the track, continue straight ahead following a **PB** sign through a metal farm gate. Go through another metal farm gate then when you come to a third, turn **RT** just before it, crossing a stile (3).

5. Walk diagonally across the field bearing 54°M over the undulating ground to steps over the wall, located about 60yds from the corner of the field. Walk in same direction through the next two fields until you emerge on an access track (4). Go through a metal farm gate on the track then over a ladder stile on your **RT**. A sign points to Castleton. Rowter Farm is just off to your **LT** now as you continue down the field.

6. Look ahead for a stile in the same direction and continue on the winding narrow grass path. Cross a step over a stone wall and continue on the grass path then over more stone steps. Keep a stone wall on your **RT** then cross a ladder stile. Walk directly to the tree at the far end of the field then to the steps over the wall by the nearby gate (5).

7. Continue over the next large field on your original track now going back to Castleton. Walk over the field in the direction of Castleton and the wood you may see ahead. You descend steeply now back on your original path down by the side of the wood then **RT** back along the stony path into Castleton.

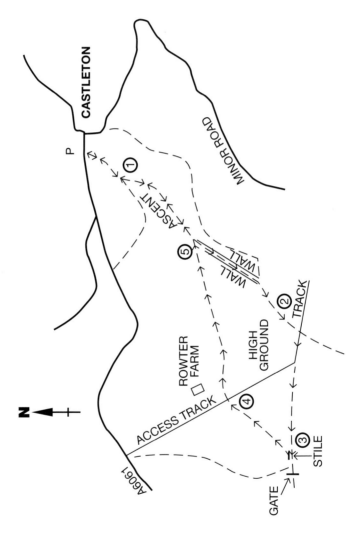

WALK 2
Not to Scale
**CASTLETON HILLS
WALK**

CASTLETON

MINOR ROAD

P

① ASCENT
ASCENT

⑤ WALL
WALL

② TRACK

ROWTER
FARM

HIGH
GROUND

ACCESS TRACK

④

A6061

N

③
STILE

GATE

Walk 3: Castleton - Hope Riverside Walk
Walk Time: 1hr 45min   **Distance 4.1miles/6.6km**
Start: GR. 149830 - Main CP in Castleton
An easy flat circular walk over fields to Hope then by the river back to Castleton.

1. From the main **CP** in Castleton, turn **LT** and ascend by the row of shops to the sharp bend by the Nags Head pub (1). Turn **LT** then at the next sharp bend continue ahead along Back Street. Continue up the **RD**, passing houses on both sides. Where the **RD** bears **LT** by an 'end of road' sign, you see Hollowford Centre (conference centre), and just to the **RT** of that is a track with signs for Rotary and **PF** (2).

2. Walk along that track between the stone walls and at a cattle grid, cross and turn immediately **RT**. Cross a field and some stepping stones over a brook then go through a gate. Continue to a small gate just past a 5-bar gate. You come to the entrance to Riding House Farm. Continue and go through a gate to emerge on a bend in the lane.

3. Turn **LT** at the bend then you come to a lane where there are five tracks all together (3). Walk straight ahead then bear **RT**. Go through a 5-bar gate beside a house, (which may be open), to emerge on a **RD**. A sign there states Lose Hill and Hope and you turn **LT** on the one-track **RD**, going through a small gate at the side of a house.

4. Just through the gate, turn immediately **RT**, behind the stables and through two small gates. Continue on the narrow path, which may be overgrown in parts. Go through another small gate into a field and turn immediately **LT** and continue into next field walking straight ahead to the far side. Go through a gate into next field keeping the hedge line on your **LT**.

5. Go through another gate, over a small **FB** and ascend a short flight of steps to another gate. Continue along the side of field with wire fence on **RT** side. Cross another small **FB** and through another gate, keeping the fence on **LT** side. At a wooden waymark post pointing to Hope, follow it across the field to a gate at the far side. Go through a kissing gate and walk round the edge of the short field.

6. Walk through a gate onto a track, then through a metal gate following a **PF** sign. Cross a stile then walk between the fence and hedge. At the end, go through a gate and ahead in front of stone buildings onto a tarmac driveway. Pass a bungalow walking ahead through a narrow opening and gate then over the railway bridge (4).

7. Emerging at the far side of a field, cross and go through a gate then through an opening into next field. Keep in same direction over fields and through gates following sign for Hope. Emerge on the **RD** with a school on your **LT**. Turn **LT** then at the junction **RT** (5) to the main **RD** through Hope. Cross to walk down by the **RT** side of the church for 300m. Continue down Tindale **RD** and ascend to a bench seat on **RT** side. Cross the stile there to walk along by the river, crossing stiles and the railway line (6) but stay in same direction.

8. Approaching Castleton, you see some houses as you follow the track to pass them (7) and emerge on the **RD** in Castleton. Turn **LT** and walk back to the village centre and **CP**.

WALK 3
Not to Scale
CASTLETON - HOPE
RIVERSIDE WALK

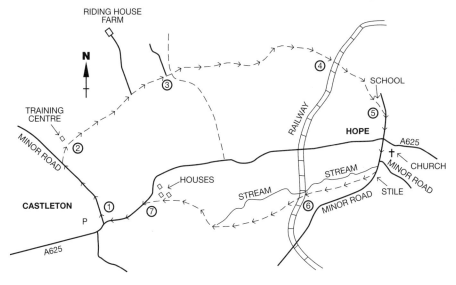

Walk 4: Roman Road/Crookstone Hill
Walk Time: 1hr 50mins   Distance 4.5miles/7.3km
Start: GR. 168847 - Fullwood Stile Lane just off Townhead Bridge.
An excellent walk with a steep ascent followed by a walk on the old Roman road along the ridge. With a gentle descent back to Townhead.

1. Park on Fullwood Stile Lane keeping well into the side to avoid blocking farm vehicles. Start from Townhead Bridge at the main **RD** and cross to the far side walking **LT** round the buildings to a sign to Lose Hill. Continue walking along the lane and take the **RT** fork (1) to pass a hotel. On reaching Oaker Farm cottages, take the **PF** to the **LT** of the cottages (2).

2. Cross two stiles there walking between the fences and over the fields. Continue in the same direction and cross the stile then bear **RT** down the track under the railway bridge to the **RD**. Cross the **RD** with care to cross a stile at the other side. Descend a path and follow it round and over Bagshaw Bridge (3).

3. Walk along the farm access **RD** and past Upper Fullwood Farm and the cottages there. Just past them, turn **RT** following the **PF** sign on a stony rutted track. Cross a stile then the track forks. Keep **RT** following the feint sign on a stone block there towards Crookstone Barn.

4. Ascend the grass and stony track then where the path forks again, take the **LT** fork ascending towards the clump of trees ahead and Crookstone Barn. The path narrows as you continue to ascend between the bracken and gorse. Cross a stile then at a broken stone wall ahead, turn **RT** (4) and ascend a stony track, going over a stile beside a metal gate and continue along the track, keeping the broken stone wall on your **LT**.

5. Approaching the trees of Woodlands Valley (5), turn **RT** over the stile following the sign to Win Hill and Hope then continue on a mostly gentle descent on the course of the old Roman road. You go through gates and ascend slightly before descending more steeply to Fullwood Stile Farm (6).

6. Approaching the farm, turn **RT** just before it, still staying on the access track, and continue descending, passing a white house on your **LT** then over the railway bridge. The track widens and becomes a metalled **RD** as you arrive at your original starting point.

WALK 4

Not to Scale

ROMAN ROAD/
CROOKSTONE HILL

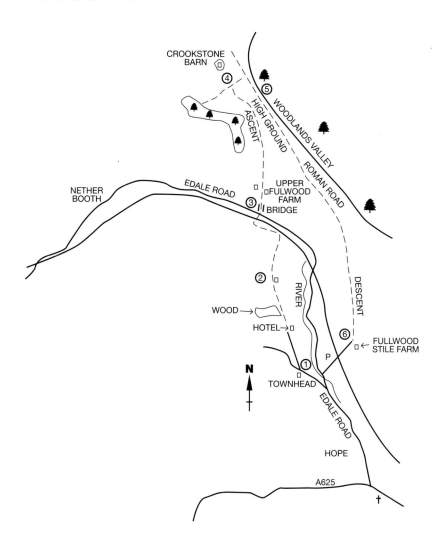

CROOKSTONE BARN

④

⑤

CROOKSTONE BARN

HIGH GROUND ASCENT

WOODLANDS VALLEY

ROMAN ROAD

NETHER BOOTH

EDALE ROAD

UPPER FULWOOD FARM

③ BRIDGE

②

RIVER

DESCENT

WOOD →

HOTEL →

⑥ FULLWOOD STILE FARM

P

N

①

TOWNHEAD

EDALE ROAD

HOPE

A625

†

Walk 5: Lose Hill Viewpoint Walk

Walk Time: 2hrs 50mins   **Distance 4.9miles/7.9km**

Start: GR. 149830 - Main CP in Castleton

A steep ascent/descent of Lose Hill then generally a flat walk after, with good views.

1. From the main **CP** in Castleton, turn **LT** and ascend by the row of shops to the sharp bend by the Nags Head pub (1). Turn **LT** then at the next sharp bend continue ahead along Back Street. Continue up the **RD**, passing houses on both sides. Where the **RD** bears **LT** by an 'end of road' sign, continue up the lane. Where the lane bends round again, look for a wooden **PF** sign on your **RT**. Take this unmade track (2) towards Only Grange Farm. Turn up towards the farm through the double metal gates.

2. Further up follow the small yellow arrow beside two stone posts, crossing a stile there and keeping the hedge line just to your **RT**. Continue straight up to the farm, crossing the stiles, ahead. When you get to the farm, go over two stiles on the **LT** side of the farmhouse then ascend the steep hillside. Continue directly to the top of the hillside where there is a stile (3).

3. Turn immediately **RT** and walk on the stony path, which ascends, keeping the fence and wood to your **RT**. Continue to the compass point on the summit of Lose Hill then descend the slabbed path at the far side (4). On reaching a stile, cross then turn **RT** to another stile. Cross this and turn **LT** to descend a grass path towards some trees (5). You come to a sign pointing to Castleton. Turn **RT** here and follow it.

4. You go through a small gate and across the next field. At another signpost stating Castleton, turn **RT** here, crossing a double stile and keep in same direction to descend a faint grass path then join a track, which leads to Losehill Farm. You come to a metal gate with a stile by it and a yellow arrow on it. Cross the stile and continue ahead. Cross a step stile by a gate then turn **LT** to descend a stony track towards Riding House Farm.

5. Cross a stile and stay on the narrow path, descending a flight of steps then going through a gate. Turn **LT** on the path and cross a stile still on the path and near the brook and trees. Go through a kissing gate and turn **RT** along an access lane (6) and at the end of the lane is **PF** sign and an opening and a gate between two stones. Go through and continue along keeping the stone wall on your **RT**.

6. Go through a gate and cross stepping-stones over the brook then walk ahead over the field onto a farm access track. Stay in the same direction on the track to pass a training and conference centre. You emerge on the minor **RD** you originally started on. Turn **LT** and walk back into Castleton then **RT** at the main **RD** back to the **CP**.

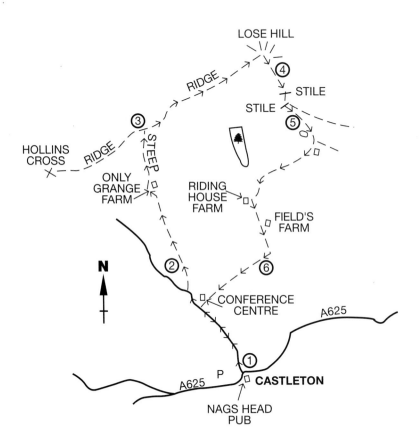

Walk 6: Vale of Edale Walk
Walk Time: 2hrs 30mins   **Distance 5.2miles/8.3km**
Start: GR. 107847 - CP near railway bridge between Upper Booth and Barber Booth.
A pleasant walk with one main ascent/descent to Hollins Cross, good views along route.

1. From the **CP** near Barber Booth, walk back under the railway bridge and stay on the **RD** to the junction with a minor **RD** (1). Walk ahead onto a **PF**, crossing a stile at the **RT** of the stone bridge and continue in the same direction over fields and stiles. At a narrow strip of woodland, carry straight through in same direction and over more fields.
2. You emerge on an access lane at Harden Clough turn **RT** and walk up the lane to a sign on **LT** stating Hollins Cross (2). Go through the wooden gate and continue on a steady ascent through several gates to Hollins Cross. Your path merges with another just before the viewpoint (3).
3. At the viewpoint, bear **LT** on a stony path between a stone and wooden post in the direction of a row of houses and a mill, back into Edale Valley. Go through a gate, still descending, towards Backtor Farm then through another gate to pass the farm on the access **RD** (4). Follow the access **RD** as it winds round, crossing the bridge over the river to the main **RD**.
4. At the **RD**, turn **RT** walking, with care on the verge, for 150yds going under the railway bridge then turning **LT** (5) along a track, which leads to Woodhouse Farm. Go through the small gate at the entrance and continue on the track to the top where it bears **LT**. Follow it round then where the track goes over a cattle grid, go straight ahead through a small gate with a yellow arrow (6).
5. Cross a series of fields, then along an access track, still in the same direction, passing houses at Nether Ollerbrook then Middle Ollerbrook. When you reach the last farm building the path forks, take the **LT** path along a track to descend into Edale. You should see the tower of Edale church ahead (7).
6. On reaching the **RD** through Edale, turn **LT**, walking past the campsite. Look for a **PF** sign on your **RT** that leads along the front of a row of cottages (8). Walk in front of the cottages then over a stile on your **LT**, taking you over the fields through openings and gates. As you approach the railway bridge (9), turn **LT** down the track taking you over the bridge and descend to the houses at Barber Booth.
7. Turn **RT** to the stone bridge over the river at the far side of the houses, then **RT** at the other side walking back along the lane where you started from, back to the **CP**.

WALK 6
Not to Scale
VALE OF EDEN WALK

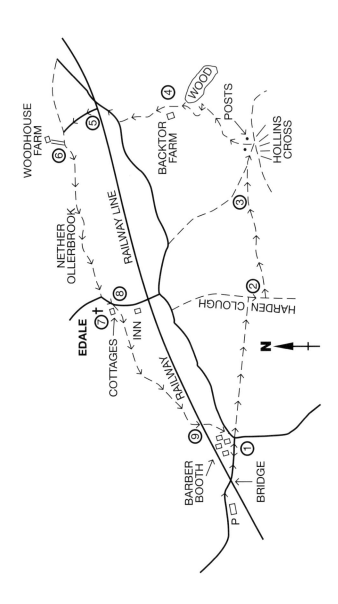

Walk 7: Caverns View Circular Walk
Walk Time: 3hrs 45mins   Distance 6.2miles/10km
Start: GR. 149830 - Main Car Park in Castleton.
A good walk with fascinating scenery and excellent views. One steep ascent/descent and one steady ascent.

1. From the main **CP** in Castleton, turn **LT** and ascend by the row of shops. Turn **RT** just past the Nags Head pub on your **RT**, and walk past the village green keeping **LT** by The Cosy Cottage tearoom then **RT** following the sign to Cave Dale. Walk between the narrow rock faces (1) and through a gate before ascending the hillside on a narrow stony path.

2. Continue ascending to the top where you see a stone wall on your **RT** side. Approaching the top, you see a gate (2) on your **RT** which you go through, walk on the path to go through another gate. You come to a broken stone wall on your **RT**, which you walk alongside. When the wall stops, bear to your **RT** to walk alongside another stone wall (3) in same direction.

3. After 100yds you come to a wooden 5-bar gate with an opening at the side. Go through then over a stone step stile soon after onto a track. Turn **RT** here on a stony track between two stone walls. When the track bends **RT** (4) continue straight ahead following a **PB** sign through a metal farm gate.

4. Go through this gate then when you come to another, turn **RT** just before it, crossing a stile to ascend the field keeping a stone wall on your **LT** side (5). At the far **LT** corner of the field, cross a stone step stile into next field and descend this field still keeping the stone wall on your **LT**. Follow the cut grass path and as you reach lower ground, you see a **RD** ahead.

5. You come to a white gate (6) leading onto the **RD**. Turn **RT** then **LT** going through a small gate by the 5-bar gate. Keep the stone wall on your **LT** as you ascend towards Mam Tor and the 'V' shape in the hillside. Stay on the main track then go through another small gate onto the main A625 **RD** (7). Cross diagonally **LT** to go through another wooden gate to ascend the grass path to the summit, going up a flight of steps.

6. On reaching the **RD** at the top, bear **RT** through a small gate, ascending steps to the summit of Mam Tor. Passing the 'trig' point, stay on the ridge (8) to Hollins Cross (round stone monument) then bear **RT** down the hill on a narrow stone slabbed path (9) which bends round. Look for the farm lower down on the **RT** as you descend and go through a gate. Take the short path bearing off **RT** taking you near the farm (10).

7. On the farm access track, go straight across through two small wooden gates and along the side of fields keeping the hedge line on your **RT**. Go through another gate then across a small **FB**. Cross two stiles together, bearing **LT** keeping a small wood on your **LT** side (11). Cross a stile by a farm gate onto an access **RD**. Turn **RT** over the stream then **LT** following a **PF** to Castleton via 'The Flatts'. Continue towards Castleton keeping the stream on your **LT**. Go through an opening and over several fields towards the houses ahead.

8. Walk through the opening between the houses onto the **RD**. Turn **LT** on the **RD** taking you back to the **CP**.

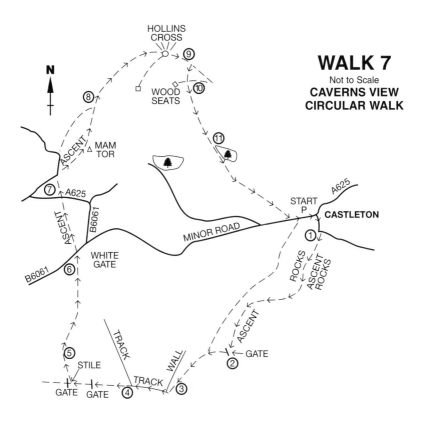

WALK 7

Not to Scale

CAVERNS VIEW CIRCULAR WALK

Walk 8: Jacobs Ladder

Walk Time: 3hrs 15mins   Distance 6.3miles/10.1km

Start: GR. 107847 - CP between Upper Booth and Barber Booth

A good walk with a short but steep ascent then a long gentle descent back.

1. Turn **LT** from the **CP** walking to Upper Booth (1). As you near the farm buildings there, continue on the narrow **RD** following sign for Jacobs Ladder. Cross the small bridge there and ascend the narrow **RD**. Go through a small gate next to a 5-bar gate following sign for Lee Farm. Stay on the access **RD** to the farm. On reaching the farm buildings, continue between them onto the rough stony track (2).

2. Cross two stiles next to 5-bar gates as you ascend the valley before coming to a gate beside a stone **FB** over the stream. Cross then ascend the stone stepped path known as Jacobs Ladder (3). At the top of the hill you come to a 5-bar gate with the Pennine Way on your **RT** and a step stile by the gate. Cross then turn immediately **LT** (4) onto a slabbed path continuing over the top of the hillside by a broken stone wall.

3. Just over the brow of the hill is another path turning off **LT** (5). Turn **LT** and walk to the 'trig' point on the highest ground at Brown Knoll then on a gradual descent over a wide expanse of open hillside. Follow the worn peat path now over level ground, which can be wet and boggy in places. You see a tower ahead, which is a ventilation shaft. Keep it well off to your **RT** as you pass, still on the path (6).

4. You join a track near a wooden post. Bear **LT** on this track (7), which soon bends round to the **RT** on a rutted track and descends the hillside going through a small gate by a 5-bar gate. Cross a step stile by another 5-bar gate then immediately **LT** through a small opening by a gate following a yellow arrow. Cross a small field diagonally, go over a stile and through a gate as you descend towards the derelict building in the valley. Behind it is Manor House Farm (8).

5. After crossing two stiles you come to an access track leading to the farm. Turn **LT** and walk to the railway bridge over the minor **RD**. At the **RD**, turn **LT** and walk back to the **CP**.

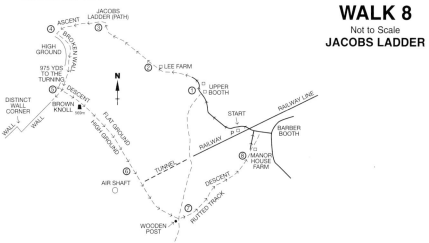

Walk 9: Rushup Ridge/Hollins Cross Circular Walk
Walk Time: 3hrs 30mins   **Distance 8.1miles/13.1km**
Start: GR. 124853 - Main Car Park in Edale
A good undulating walk with excellent views and one steep ascent/descent.

1. Turn **RT** from the main **CP** in Edale and walk under the railway bridge into the village. On reaching the Old Nags Head pub, turn **LT**, following a sign for Upper Booth (1).

2. Go through a kissing gate then another gate further up as you ascend the path. You come to a stile on **LT**, signposted for Upper Booth. Cross and walk on a slabbed path, going through two openings into fields (2). Cross stone steps over the wall into a further field.

3. Continue around the hillside through a small wooden gate on the obvious path then over stone steps again. At a sign for Crowden Clough/Jacobs Ladder, follow Jacobs Ladder **LT**. Descend the hillside, cross a stile then through a small gate, still descending gently into the valley.

4. Cross a stile, continue on the rutted track crossing another stile by a 5-bar gate. You are now at Upper Booth (3) as you walk between the farm buildings and descend the winding path between them and past a post box. At the lower end of the farm go straight across on a narrow path just to the **RT** of the telephone box.

5. Cross a small **FB** into a copse and ascend the far side to cross a stile out of it. You emerge in a grass field with a farm ahead. A stone step stile is just to the **RT** of it. Cross then bear **RT** up the embankment to a gate. Continue across the next field to a metal farm gate by a barn. Keep the stone wall on your **LT** as you cross the undulating hillside and drop down to a ladder stile.

6. Cross and descend by a wood, keeping the stone wall just to your **LT**. Cross fields and two further stiles approaching the railway line/tunnel. At a house called 'The Orchard' (4) you drop down to cross the **FB** and over a stile onto an unmade track.

7. Cross the track following a sign for Whitemoor Clough, through a small gate keeping the stone wall just to your **LT**. Cross a stile where your path bends **RT** then **LT**, to cross a brook. Stay on path to a stile leading into a field with a barn. Walk to far side of the barn and cross a stile. You are now at the base of a hill. Ascend the hill; you come to a rutted track after a short distance.

8. Turn **RT** on this track and follow it to the ridge along the top of the hill. Another track joins from the **RT** but continue ahead. On meeting a definite path (5), running **RT** to **LT**, turn **LT** and follow this path for 1.7miles and cross a stile to emerge on a **RD** between the hillsides (6). Turn **LT** then **RT** at a bus stop and go through a gate following a rutted track up the hillside. Your path merges with the path descending from the summit.